DINOSAUR RELATIVES

by Janet Riehecky
illustrated by Diana Magnuson

THE
CHILD'S
WORLD

MANKATO, MN

*Grateful appreciation is expressed to
Bret S. Beall, Research Consultant,
Field Museum of Natural History, Chicago,
Illinois, who reviewed this book to
insure its accuracy.*

Library of Congress Cataloging in Publication Data

Riehecky, Janet, 1953-
    Dinosaur relatives / by Janet Riehecky ; illustrated by Diana
Magnuson.
        p. cm. — (Dinosaur books)
    Summary: Describes other reptiles that were alive during the age
of dinosaurs, including creatures that lived in the sea and those
that flew through the skies.
    ISBN 0-89565-626-4
    1. Reptiles, Fossil—Juvenile literature.   [1. Reptiles, Fossil.]
I. Magnuson, Diana, ill.   II. Title.   III. Series: Riehecky, Janet,
1953-   Dinosaur books.
QE861.R47   1990
567.9—dc20   90-43744
                                                                    CIP
                                                                    AC

1 2 3 4 5 6 7 8 9 10 11 12 R 98 97 96 95 94 93 92 91 90

DINOSAUR RELATIVES

During the age of dinosaurs, more than 350 different kinds of dinosaurs lived. They ruled every inch of the land. Nothing got in their way!

But dinosaurs did not live in the ocean
or in the sky. Other reptiles ruled in these
places. These reptiles were relatives of the
dinosaurs, but they were not dinosaurs.

The reptiles that lived in the sea were just as strange and unusual as their cousins, the dinosaurs. Some were huge creatures, as large as whales. Most were fierce meat eaters, with long, sharp teeth and big appetites. They ruled their watery world just as fiercely as the dinosaurs ruled theirs.

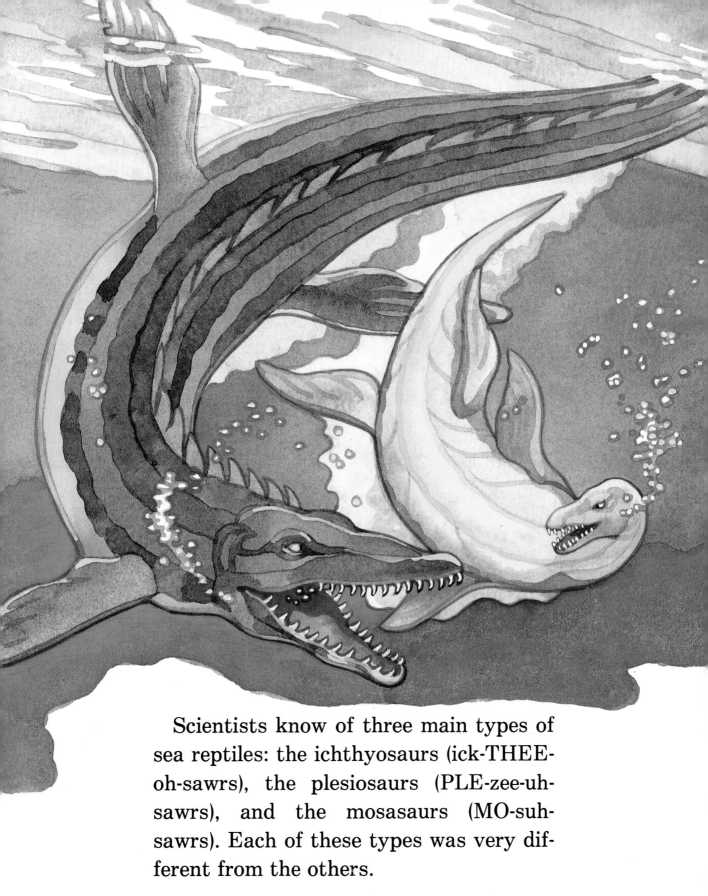

Scientists know of three main types of sea reptiles: the ichthyosaurs (ick-THEE-oh-sawrs), the plesiosaurs (PLE-zee-uh-sawrs), and the mosasaurs (MO-suh-sawrs). Each of these types was very different from the others.

Ichthyosaurs were very much like fish. In fact, their name means "fish lizard." They had streamlined bodies, fins, and even fishlike tails. But the ichthyosaurs were not fish. Fish breathe through gills which can take oxygen directly out of water. Ichthyosaurs had lungs. They had to poke their heads above the surface of the water to get air to breathe.

Scientist think ichthyosaurs could swim very fast. They were shaped a lot like the modern tuna, which can swim at speeds faster than twenty-five miles per hour. Being able to swim that fast would have helped ichthyosaurs catch fish and other sea creatures.

Ophthalmosaurus

Mixosaurus

There were many different kinds of ichthyosaurs. An early one was called the Mixosaurus (MIX-oh-sawr-us). It had long jaws lined with many sharp teeth. Another, later type, was the Ophthalmosaurus (off-THAL-mo-sawr-us). It had enormous eyes, which might have helped it hunt in the dark.

One of the most famous ichthyosaurs was the Ichthyosaurus, which gave its name to the whole group of fishlike reptiles. Scientists know a lot about the Ichthyosaurus because of the many, remarkable fossils they have found of it, including over a hundred skeletons. Some of the fossils show the actual shape of the Ichthyosaurus' body. The fins, the tail, and other soft parts of the body all left detailed impressions in the rock.

Even more remarkable are some fossils showing female Ichthyosaurs appearing to give birth! Most reptiles lay eggs, but these fossil skeletons show Ichthyosaurs delivering live babies in the sea. How that moment came to be preserved in rock will never be completely known, but it is amazing to be able to catch such a glimpse into the life of this long-dead creature.

Plesiosaurs, the second type of sea reptile, were not as fish-like as the ichthyosaurs. The name plesiosaur means "nearly like a lizard." Most, but not all, plesiosaurs had big, thick, barrel-like bodies, very long, snake-like necks, small heads with large eyes, and flippers instead of legs.

Plesiosaurs lived most of their lives in
the water. But scientists think they could
crawl out of the water on their bellies.
They could push themselves along with
their flippers as sea turtles do today. Why
would they do this when they could move

so much more easily in the water? Well,
plesiosaurs, unlike ichthyosaurs, did lay
eggs. And reptile eggs cannot survive in
sea water. Plesiosaurs had to make their
difficult journey in order to lay their eggs
on the land.

There were many different types of plesiosaurs. The Elasmosaurus (ee-LAZ-mo-sawr-us) was one of the strangest. It had a neck almost as long as a city bus! It could swim along, darting its head quickly in any direction, catching even the fastest-moving fish.

The Kronosaurus (KRO-no-sawr-us) was one of the fiercest plesiosaurs. It had a very short neck and a large head with powerful jaws and very sharp teeth. It was probably just as ferocious as the Tyrannosaurus.

The third type of sea reptile, the mosasaurs, were the most ferocious of all. Named for the Meuse River where they were found, these huge creatures terrorized the seas. They had powerful tails, long, slender bodies, short necks, and long heads. Their jaws were lined with sharp, vicious teeth. These were true sea monsters, feeding on any other animal that crossed their path. The largest mosasaur was the Tylosaurus (TIE-lo-sawr-us). It was about as big as a great white shark—and just as fierce.

While these reptiles ruled the seas, other reptiles ruled the skies. The pterosaurs (TAIR-oh-sawrs) or "winged lizards" lived throughout the age of dinosaurs.

Pterosaurs were lightly-built creatures with small bodies and large eyes. They had three clawed fingers on each hand and a fourth, enormously long finger which supported their wings. The wings came in many sizes. Some were as small as a sparrow's. One type had wings as large as an airplane's.

Scientists have found two main types of pterosaurs: rhamphorhynchs (RAM-for-INKS) and pterodactyls (TAIR-uh-DAK-tiles).

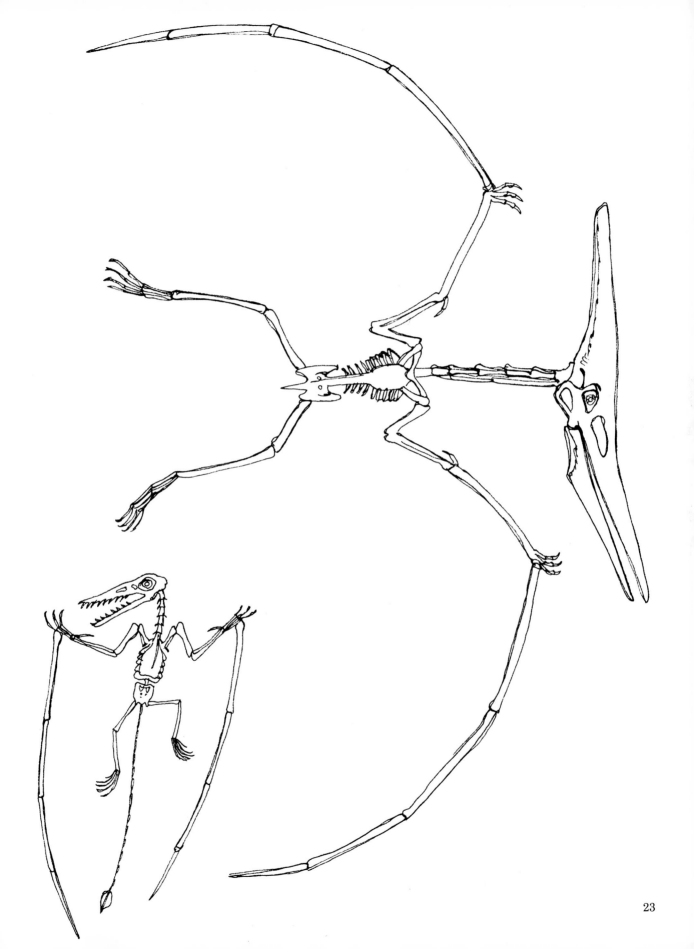

Rhamphorhynchs had large heads, short necks, and long tails with "paddles" at the end. Most of them had many sharp, pointed teeth. Scientists have found evidence that at least some of them were covered with hair three inches long!

Rhamphorhynchs were strange-looking creatures. One of them, the Dimorphodon (die-MORF-oh-don) had an eight-inch head on a six-inch body. Another, the Dorygnathus (Do-ree-NATH-us), had very long, sharp teeth that stuck out of its mouth.

The best known rhamphorhynch was the Rhamphorhynchus. Its body was about the size of a pigeon, but its wings stretched out four-feet wide. Its tail was almost twice as long as its entire body. Scientists think it lived close to the seashore. They picture it swooping down over the water, snatching fish with its dagger-like teeth. The paddle at the end of its tail would have helped it change directions quickly as it chased its victims.

The first pterodactyls appeared fifty million years after the first rhamphorhynchs. For a while, both types of creatures ruled the skies, but gradually all the rhamphorhynchs died out. The pterodactyls were better at flying than the rhamphorhynchs. Their large wings were made to help them soar gracefully through the skies. The typical pteradactyl had a long, slender body, a long, curved neck, and a very small tail. Many pteradactyls were toothless, but some of them had some of the strangest teeth you can imagine.

One pteradactyl was named Cteno-
chasm (TEN-oh-KAZ-um), which means
"comb mouth." It had hundreds of sharp,
needle-like teeth in its mouth, just like a
comb.

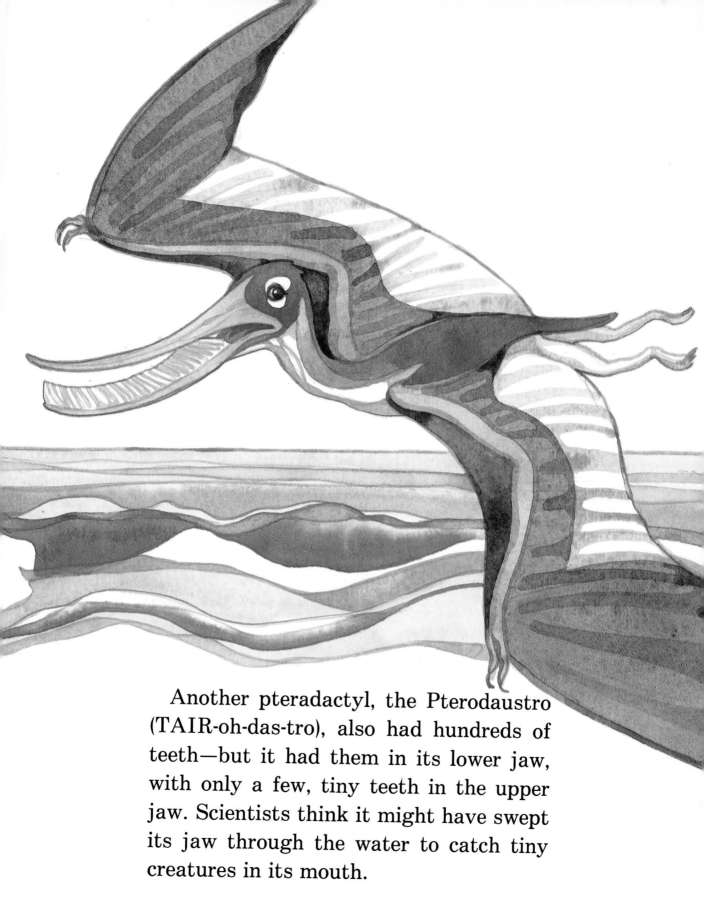

Another pteradactyl, the Pterodaustro
(TAIR-oh-das-tro), also had hundreds of
teeth—but it had them in its lower jaw,
with only a few, tiny teeth in the upper
jaw. Scientists think it might have swept
its jaw through the water to catch tiny
creatures in its mouth.

One of the largest pteradactyls was the Pterandon (ter-AN-oh-don). Its body was only about the size of a turkey's, but its wings stretched out thirty feet wide. The Pteranodon had a strange crest on its head, making its head six feet long. Scientists don't know why it had that large crest. It might had helped the Pterandon steer, or it might have helped the Pteranodon attract a mate.

The largest pteradactyl ever found—in fact, the largest flying creature ever known—was the Quetzalcoatlus (KWET-zohl-ko-AHT-lus). This enormous creature was as big as an airplane. Its wings stretched out fifty feet wide!

Some of these flying and swimming reptiles died out before the end of the age of dinosaurs. None of the ones described in this book lived past the end of that age. Whatever killed all the dinosaurs killed them too. Some reptiles, of course, do live on today, such as snakes, lizards, turtles, and crocodiles. But no longer do reptiles rule the skies or the seas.

Dinosaur Fun

What would you do if you saw an Ichthyosaur washed up on the beach? That's not likely, but the next time you're at the beach you can make your own beached Ichthyosaur—with sand. You'll probably need help from a friend or two. And shovels and buckets will help you gather the huge pile of sand you'll need to make this giant dinosaur relative! Follow the pictures in this book to build your model. You may want to use stones or shells for the eyes. When you're all done, don't forget to take a picture to help you remember the day you discovered a beached Ichthyosaur!